CW00404453

ONCE WE CARVED ANGELS

ONCE WE
CARVED ANGELS

Tom Barry

GOLDEN
GUTTER
PRESS

WINSOR
HAMPSHIRE
ENGLAND

First published in Great Britain by Golden Gutter Press in 2007

Golden Gutter Press
Winsor
Hampshire
England

British Library Cataloguing-in Publication data
A catalogue record for this book is available from the British Library

ISBN-10: 0-9526163-1-9
ISBN-13: 978-0-9526163-1-3

Typeset and Printed in Great Britain by CPI Antony Rowe,
Bumpers Farm, Chippenham, Wiltshire

To those who live with the memories.
To those who sometimes tried to explain *Why*.
Those who want nothing to be forgotten.

The last time I saw my grandfather
he held a knife with a strong curving blade
his left hand holding the block of wood steady
the hard fingers wrapped over the heads
of his neighbour and one of her children
drawing the knife slowly towards him

Autumn sunlight
dropped through the reddening leaves
of the plum tree on to the dust
of last winter's dried mud

where he sat on a broken chair
arguing with the old woman his wife
over some ancient memory or other
the sunlight on his bared head silvering
the grey, purpling his cheekbone
whitening the woodchips in dust round his feet

Another Place

I write this to you in morning's half-light
in the cold shadow left of yesterday's shape
and I am searching for words
                       with which to build fire
a cave of warmth for the now homeless spirit

We drove all day to reach names of places
long empty miles under darkening clouds
warm in our seats as the road scrambled on
toward the next name rarely stopping the car

We drove as I say through names of places
black timbers that shone in the sun like plum blossom
fields of tall grass all empty of cattle
as once Eden was with Adam cast out.

There is no horizon here
that's not abrupt
mountain forest field
their meetings marked
with the hard definition
of national borders

I suppose, in many ways
I should feel at home
for these sort of raw edges
remind me of Canada
where people carve their way
back into wilderness

But this is Europe
old long-settled land
where men have had centuries
to smooth and blend, and
the harsh nature of it ought
by now to have been mastered

Flowers hide the story of the soil
you told me once, explaining how
what shapes it – raised it, smoothed it down
is all hid now by fields and woods
so we shan't see what work we stand upon

You spoke of mighty primal force
the heaving thrust of molten fire
of the spilling forth, and death of seas
then bitter cold, the grind of ice
of countless unseen silent springs
milleniums of rain and drought

But here, today, it's subtler marks
for which we search – grassed-over ruts
and here not flowers but fresh sprung weeds
where men have broken through Earth's past
to malform that story by a lie.

Broken chalk thrown up
when the land was ploughed?

or a last patch of snow
held in a drift of leaves?

a bough of plum blossom
in an old saki bottle
its petals fallen
on the black wood?

... scraps of white paper
children's torn drawings
scattered over a playground
crumpled, rain trodden?

What the eye thinks it sees
in the rank shadows
the first green growth
held in an empty eye socket

These houses, empty just a year
already smell of long decay
an earthy damp of fungal wood
of plaster rot and sour stale soot

kitchen cupboards stink of mice
taps drip rust into cracked sinks
toilets rimmed with yellow dirt
when no one flushed a final crap

jammed doors scrape open on to rooms
where ceiling trail long webs of dust
to carpets patterned with white mould
walls the plaster flaking off

behind cracked glass a photo curls
a red plastic toy lies on a chair
and from somewhere close but yet unseen
there sounds the busy drone of flies.

The metal arm draws back
the driver, leaning from his cab
jabs his fist towards the hole
wet clay
dribbles from the bucket high above

I stand closer to the edge to see
what may have been uncovered now
here in this third pit of the day
gouged in this quiet meadow
overhung by summer trees

leaves print patterns on the marl
and in the slants of evening sun
dancing midges rise and fall

beyond the diesel's idling tick
fresh birdsong welcomes lessening heat
loose clods of turf which break away
splash down upon the sky below.

A thing each of us noticed was how
little their shoes appeared changed
by the months of burial, even in clay

Today we have moved some forty miles
across the mountains to a different season
and a fine cold rain

glistening the walls of the excavation
to sparkle pebble jewels alive
and grease this clay we slide our way through
to follow the work of those who dig
back into the banks of loosened soil

These young men, the age of my children
who climb the ladder to walk away up the hill
taking off their gloves
and who kneel in the gently falling rain
to wipe their hands on the clean bright grass

Whoever painted
the cross on the door of this house
a looped scrawl of red
in thick paint used on machinery
splashed it on with a heavy brush
so that dribbles follow the grain of wood
to congeal upon the threshold
like globules of blood

What
did it signify
at the moment of doing?

... the Nazi mark slashed
across all those doors of the Ghettos
of Europe
                    Here Live Juden!

Or was it just maybe
the signal that Moses
told his people to make on their own doors
so the Angels of Death would know
                    and pass by.

On the road outside they're kicking ball
the thud of boots upon taut skin
and the sharp explosive shouts
of young men who've had tension stored

This morning we stood by to watch
as the town re-buried its lost sons
bodies yesterday recovered
from a midden of still steaming dung
Hundreds in the crowd who followed
their coffins through this hate-torn place
jeered at emptied muslim houses
and as they passed a burnt-out mosque
From his church steps a priest harangued them
like some fearsome desert prophet
delivering Jehovah's warning!
It seemed wise to pull our people back
and leave our business till tomorrow

Saddened seeing such blind hatred
yet in this mob were genuine mourners
young girls who never raised their head
stricken mothers broken fathers
and old men stumbling after boxes
that held for them a cruel reversal
their future's death though they still live.

These men who stand to bar our way
in farmers' heavy work stained clothes
clumsy boots with dried on dirt
their hands hooked under rifle slings
buckled by hard years of work
lounge in easy confidence
the challenging untroubled stare
of hunters home-bound from the hill
of lovers wearied by their day

I search in eyes for signs of what?
some signal spark, a warning flare
flickering far back in their night
to betray a pulse of madness here!
Yet nothing in this level gaze
tells these are the eyes of killers.

Why not call me – Frankenstein?
his humour leaves him much amused
He smiles across the polished desk
Yes, *Doctor* Frankenstein will do!

Healthy, strong, his manner smoothed
by professional power, his confidence
displayed in well kept hands and teeth
he is at ease to show he needn't care
a damn what I may think of him

He gives the list a cursory glance
No – no you won't find any here!
he holds his hand back for the notes
the waiting nurse lays onto it
Let's see? Ah yes – a single ward
of women, mostly old. And some
sick children – but no men!

No wounded men?
                              No Muslim men!

again he smiles across the desk
on which a vase of fresh spring flowers
stands beside photos of his wife and kids
He holds his gaze out-staring mine
They find another place for them!

'. . . in the cellar there were women's clothes.
Also a man's shirt, slashed and stained. In a
sack further stained clothing, and a driving-
*licence with the name ********* *********
There were no human remains in the house or
the farm buildings. In the yard the bodies
of several dead cattle.'

No need to hide the corpses since no one
will be arraigned at The Hague for killing cows
so leave them as you slew them months ago

at first they would have swelled to obscene size
enough to show in photos from the sky
enlarged again on someone's monitor

as gases leaked they sank back on themselves
their juices leached to stain the earth around
maggots fed on through the summer months

given time, nature would have reabsorbed
them to become constituents of grass
leaving flat hide and slowly crumbling bone

hauled out to be buried now they weigh
so light one man can drag along a cow
dead clothing lasting better than they do.

Obsidian blades cut
as neatly as fine steel
in the hands of those
who know anatomy:
the points where bones
knit to their sockets,
the layering of tissue
sheathing muscles,
the centre line of ribs
above the heart.

One of the greatest skills of torture
was to flay alive a human being
inch by careful inch
removing the whole skin.
It must have required the most delicate
of touches
and a special kind of imagination.

In Japan the art of food preparation
can attain heights of skill
honoured beyond poetry or painting.
Stunning the epicure
with a razor knife and the most delicate
of touches
the maestro serves the gasping fish
carved in a hundred slivers.

Why be
troubled with these flies
that do such a business for us
and left alone for long enough
will do it so well
that we may reach and casually
pick up a human bone
as impersonal as
a whitened bough of a fallen tree.

Funerals

Should be held in the open air
amid the usual business of the town
its commerce and its casual inattention
the breath of the world passing
to hurry the soul on its way

And the body ought not
to be immolated
in a steel casement of mechanical fire
but raised on a sunlit mirage of heat
in a haze of scented wood-smoke shaping
a faintest lightening of the surrounding air

Burial

And got by with quickly
like an event in the weather
without long-drawn explanation
or ceremony with strangers

Beneath a spreading tree
with just a few gathered
for this one last duty of love:
breaking earth with a spade

And any words to be said
should be spoke without rehearsal
and the flowers ought to be sown
so they will bloom fresh on the grave

For a headstone

Always use
whatever lies to hand
In the mountains rock
In the forest wood

If wood, starting with a fresh shake
split bright that morning with an axe
shape it rough then smooth it so
the blade will not jump holding the curve
of your hand around lettering and date

In the night to follow, taking time
by lamplight, as shavings flare the fire
with a sharp knife whittle out
those plain facts in which a life is told
Watched by the dog
  who knows, yet doesn't understand
carve this last avowal of your love...

Warmed now by coffee
                    I walk out
in star night frost
boot squeak of snow
falling all day to cover up
the ruts cut by our lorry wheels
smooth away the shape of things

The storm moved on an hour or so
to leave no Moon, the night so dark
I move with the edges of my eyes
between the loom of walls and trees
all moisture frosted from the air
a night as clear as crystal glass
I move ahead below a river of fire!

Immensity of blazing suns
more stars than any mind can hold
that make nonsense of all pain and hope
a Universe beyond all reasoning

at the most
          a speck of dust
to flare a moment in the night.

I read his words
           So old
yet new each time
I open up this book
         and often think
Two Thousand years ago
one man knew everything
we'll ever know

        Dressed perhaps
in miracles and such as
was reckoned needed then
to secure a foothold with
established myth

         Later they
compressed a body round this
youthful joyous confidence
and corpulence and age
have done the rest

Afterwards
there is the shock out of season
the collateral damage to loved ones
adjustment of terms at the end of a crisis
a lost sense of purpose, need of new reasons

but first, we need space
space and time, time for forgetfulness
some sun warmed corner, somewhere
to watch the grass coming straight again

And, today,
in the slush of an Ottowa spring
I start to forget how winter
has tied down this land
for so long now it seems
that grasses and flowers
were a country elsewhere
a place I once visited.

Picnic at Tusla

They come on an outing
these women and girls in bright summer frocks
climbing down from the dust-covered bus
standing a moment dazed by the sunlight
holding the hands of little children

They arrive, bus following bus
from a haze of dust and distance
windows blanked with silent faces
mirages becoming solid
into a dream, having come from reality

And stand now waiting to be ordered
towards, into, or just to wait
with no purpose here except survival
for what is left of what was theirs

At last, each gathering her bundles
and her children to her seeks a wall
and spreading in its narrow shade
a quilt snatched – only yesterday? –
from the bed she's slept in half her life
begins to open up her parcels
finding mostly only useless things
ornaments and photographs
some scented soap wrapped in a veil
things that have no present meaning
...shoes she once wore to a dance

And remembers she has left behind
a fridge with butter milk and eggs
coffee sugar loaves of bread
fresh water gushing from a tap
and now fastens on such simple losses
to hold the greater horror back.

outside the wire the poppy flower
moves lightly to a passing truck

outside the wire a water tap
drips in the dust

this side the pipe is cut
and hammered to a knot

this side nothing happens much
birds fly into view, then go

the sun burns down on shuffled dust
sometimes at night a wind blows through

sometimes at night the voices call
the names of those who are not here

at night in dreams we still are men
dawn hollows us to dust once more

outside the wire a paper bag
drifts idly down the empty road

the tap drips in its pit of mud
the poppy shivers now and then

this land is hard land this land
is all bone and no flesh this land's

trees grow from rock and its
waters flow thick as ancient oil

this land's people come from God knows
where embedded in it like ironstone

this land
has faiths like foxstink

and its pride is rooted like cancer
and its earth stiffened with blood

this land its people are
farmers and poets peasants and painters

zealots and wood-carvers singers and
myth-shapers who

make blood in to wine.

I've never thought a road much good
in winter washed out, blocked by snow

in summer potholes, choking dust
and travel always long and hard

when a girl I walked behind a cow
or through cold mud to get to school

later a road took me to town
my father's tractor fetched me home
and soon marriage kept me prisoner

I didn't mind, I knew a road
would never bring me any good

This road now, where's it taking us
I keep asking them but they won't say

it seems to me that they don't know?
I know only what it takes away!

this road is bad, all roads are bad
ahead? behind? how far? how long!

in summer rain fell
as pure relief

patterning leaves
with rivulets of dust

easing air
into our lungs

bringing the horizon
to focus again

for months now this
cold driving rain

has nailed
clothes to my body

blanched all
life from our skins

and leached away our
last courage and hope

Trapped by the roadblock now she stands
pressing down the shoulders of her son

to make him stoop, hissing fiercely
Bend your knees!

She curses now the many prayers
she has offered for his lengthening bones

that he should grow up tall and straight
fleshed with the hardness of a man

Aches now for that easy light
of slim small bones, the slender neck

the fingers of his hands like girls
the childish prattle of his voice

before it broke in to a man's
Now hates herself for her delight

in watching him grow tall and broad
filling out his father's clothes

Will give herself, pay any price
to these men who now so casually choose

those they sweep by with their guns
and who they haul out take away.

outside the mosque they talk of jews
my father a brave man used to say

they went to their death like helpless sheep
queued into the wagons without a fight

for me? with nothing left to lose
I would have done my best to kill a kraut!

Yet when our own turn came we stood like sheep
we went this way or that as we were told

watched them prod our men onto their trucks
sons and husbands, watched them take them all

knowing what would happen, knew it must!
gasped like breath the light out of our souls

it seemed our frozen brains could find no reason
to make a sacrifice of what was left

and he, the brave one, his hair gone white
took one step forward one step back

then raised his hand a little to his sons
as they went into the forest, out of sight

Raindrops falling leaf to leaf
made these pits in summer dust

Tears which fell then dried
left the scars on these cheeks

A bed of arid whitened stone
twisted by the roots of trees

where soft spring water flowed
in the shade of tender leaves

A bank of unbruised grass
fresh-dewed in the morning sun

is now contused, torn open raw
to hold the thistle seed.

After thirty years of talk
what is there left to say

Wife and husband talking
with less need to every day

Your face become stolid
its quick suppleness now stiff

My body grown thickened
useful muscle for soft flesh

I shall miss my garden
the hens coming to my door

And you... no word is spoken
hands touching nothing more.

What use is a tongue
when nothing has meaning

When all words have failed
to find an ear to listen

What good is love
if all love loses its power

to save what is loved
another hour

Fire burned you black
ate away your lips and ears

it made a crater of your nose
and crisped your hair to orange moss

it shrank your eyelids back to bone
it fired your eyes to pearly stone

and yet they did not burst?
it ate deep in your gentle breast

and smoking melten wool and skin
shrank tight around all that was left

and yet this smouldering log moved
and with its lipless mouth it made

a sound of love and sympathy.

without iman or priest
I lay my life in this grave

with no weakness for grief
the clay falls from this spade

with no coffin but a sheet
to cover your face

your hand held this last moment
let go nothing left

do not forget
before anger dies

to throw this rock
of hate

do not forgive
before pain dulls

the cruelty
of grief

do not wish
to find some ease

in mercy
or with Faith

how stupid to think
passion would leave

with age marks on skin
when my hair became thin

when those parts of my body
I pressed with such need

grew slackened through use
when I dried in my juice

how wrong was I then
how wrong was I then

The eye staggers on this line
of portraits fastened to the wall
by different hands, is jerked
along from face to face
skipping detail, gaining only
an impression of how young most are
and with what shining confidence
they face their future in the camera

So that all who now press in the door
are made to halt, and stand confused
at the brightness of this welcome
as if they have come without due warning
upon an unexpected party
and need a moment to refind themselves
and reaffirm their purpose here
before they can start their crabwise shuffle
along this line of snapshot prints
pausing to focus now and then
when one appears they almost know
and have to stand up close to certain
the camera has not lied some feature?

A woman halts, no need, she **knows**
recognising certain truth . . .

She reaches with a shaking hand
to touch the image, drawing down
her fingers on the face
speaks to the photograph by name
smooths a buckled corner back in place

then turns
acknowledging at last
the truth that will not be denied
to her husband's shoulder, lays her head
unmoving silently they stand
a grounded iceberg in the crowd
that dividing round them shuffles on
before the smiles of those who wait
with timeless confidence for life.

'Once we carved Angels'

At four the bucket is put into your hand
you lean your small body against its weight
the iron handle bites into your palm
you squeeze the dust between your toes
It never flows uphill does water

I was about seven maybe
rolling under the kitchen table
into a mess of blind mewing kittens
and a puddle of afterbirth

Too many damned cats, grandfather said
Too many damn cats!
I went off to school
When I came home old cat
and her last kittens were gone

Days later
in the disused well
I found the string going down
into the murk... to a sack
weighted with drowned cats
snarling white lips, claws torn

Now, years after
turning over the soil
I dig up a mess of fine bones
tangled like wire
... and puzzle a moment
a skein of bones, nothing more.

The playground, when you're new
is where it starts

Between bullied and bulliers you form gangs
and discover the first teaching of survival
to be different is lonely, worse it's odd

So from now, for the rest, you'll tell
them lies
        about yourself the *who* you really are
Survival you have learnt is compromise

Look at you now – you dirty old woman
black grains in your skin, thick broken nails
and hair like the strands of coarse sisal twine
you use to tie the calf to its bucket

What are you – humpback matted with straw
bruise on your neck where the prong-handle pressed
and your flat knotted feet spread wide in the yard
as you cackle the chickens scattering corn

What are you – who now treats herself
as no special thing, of less use than the horse
that can haul wagon or plough
less worth than a cow that can still fall to calf
More like the dog, who is half-blind and deaf
and now needs the fire as much as you do
you two the guardians of the other's old age

Look at you – who still rise from habit
filling the kettle on your way to the outhouse
plashing handcups of water to your face and your crotch
everything grizzled that was once silken soft

Look at you, who has worked the years of your body
in to this soil you have made of your flesh.

They're handing out the rifles like the vote
making us responsible and proud
that now we have the power to fix our future!
Choose a leader Grab a truck, and follow us!

It's hard to find a reason why we shouldn't
though most of us aren't that keen to go
there's supper on the table, wives are waiting
But when someone finds a lorry up we get
and holding our new guns and one another
away we roar, unexplained, into the night
What's on? Where to? Gods knows?

We follow the lights ahead for half an hour
tearing through other places on the road
in most of them the houses all in darkness
not sleeping yet but trying to look they are

We stop and scramble down and stand around
not really sure just what we're doing here
I know this place we sometimes play them football
farmers mostly much the same as us

A SHOT! another! then another!
a fusillade!
                    sparks flying off the walls!
we're shooting-up the houses dogs are howling
we all shoot and yell now the screaming starts

66

in the headlamps now we see them running
men and women old ones little kids
staring back the fierce light on their faces
in panic to find darkness if they can

somebody hands me a tank of petrol
so I smash a window slosh it round inside
toss in a match and jump back when it *whooshes!*
move to the next till every window's red
the barns catch hold I hear the cattle blaring
in swirling smoke the stench of burning hair
as roofs fall in great sparks go flying upwards!
night turns red like a Christmas feast
We stand around and watch until it's over
then drive back to our own place to our village.

It hits me – how thin
the skin's been on my *proper strength*
power always in me, but kept tied
by the fears of women and their priests!

You *know it* with the gun's weight in your hand
and grow with it – it makes you twice the man!

And nothing beats it – *Nothing* – even drunk
I never got to feel this kind of free

Knowing how at last I've got the strength
to grab the World and make it come to me

Slam my boots down hard upon *my* earth
And drink hot metal out of *my own* sky

Back in town they think it smart
to keep a dog to walk the English way
The ones with money they import their hounds
get them clipped and even have them dyed
then stroll them up and down between the cafes
those *Daddy's girls* – nice dog nice fuck, we'd say

Out here the bloody things are more like wolves
given half a chance these buggers will have you
go for your face or sneak in from behind
to tear and rip before you guess they're there

Only one thing scares 'em – it's a gun
they'll snarl a bit before they run away
or cower dragging their bellies in the mud
whining panting making out we're friends

If the first shot doesn't kill they set to howl
and Arvy who's a bastard breaks their backs
just above the pelvis – and stands grinning
as the front half bites its backside, it's his way

Now we drive in through the ruins of
our bombardment, seeing how the earth's
all smashed, the corn laid dying flat
the cattle stiff-legged swollen by the roadside
their bloated udders spilling milk
blackened hay smoulders on the rickpoles
shattered orchards scattered fruit
dead dogs beside the buildings, chicken feathers
blown about by breeze as we drive through
But soil' s good here we farmers notice
and barns are holed yet look to be wellbuilt
houses will need fixing, roofs retiling
Sure there' s work to do but nothing we shan't fix!

You ride a sow
to find if she'll stand to the boar
A heifer bellows when she sees the bull
and pulls hard back against the halter
rolls her eyes up white and bawls again
as he slams his weight down into her
but after she's as quiet as a nun

These women yell
and cry when they're held down
and twist their bodies every way they can
spit up in to you face or try to bite you
There's some won't have it even then
unless they're beaten to a bloody quiet

That's war – I tell my lads – *that's war*
their fault for being what and where they are.

Without need of it we tell them lies
All older boys and men will go to camps
not caring or expecting they'll believe it

Yet they seize on our words like drowning men
grasping at their last mouthful of bubbles
desperate to claw their way back to the surface
scrambling to haul themselves up on the truck
like it's giving them a final hope of freedom

But their women aren't fooled by it a second
and start up that ghastly moaning wail
that grates your nerves and has their husbands
looking down at us to shrug embarrassed
One calls 'Don't make such fuss be quiet
carrying on will only make things worse!'
but they've guessed the truth and keep up howling
throwing themselves down clutching at the dirt
and beat their faces crawling trying
to get near enough to kiss our boots

We kick them back start up the lorry
drive a short way to a track into a wood
and up it till we reach a bit of clearing
full of rubbish old stuff rotting in the sun
Ordered to they climb down silent
then shuffle where we tell them standing there
pressing close and staring at the ground
or look around at green leaves and the sky
nobody protests or needs to question
what's going to happen now ... some start to pray
the older men put arms around the youngest.

It startles you how fast a man
who moments back could meet your look
with eyes holding all that life and panic
hope and hate that makes a human work
whose shirt shows where a thudding heart
is sending warm life racing to his brain
desperate with a thousand thoughts a moment
is turned as sudden as a switched off light
to a jerking, then a settling heap
of clothing like a shapeless sack
thrown to the grass ... where others fall
and mould themselves together while yet soft
to a formlessness, soon hardening to a lump.

What's real becomes more like a dream
though dreams can sometimes seem more real
than blood that kicks up from these shirts
at times more like a fairground game
than targets who are living men
stumbling to clothed lumps of flesh
Nothing's real
                    except we move
with angry joy across this land
to redeem it from an ancient curse
to purify our roots again.

What's up? he says These boots! I say
– these fuggin boots are killing me!
and show him how they're rubbing raw
clear through the socks, my bloodied feet
Don't worry, you'll soon wear them in
he says and laughs *They'll wear me in!*
I say We laugh

We've dragged the tarp up to the truck
and he calls Hey Fartarse take your time
and we watch his backside backing out
Is this the last? he's reaching down
to grab a corner Christ they stink!
We could have left them where they are!
we heave it up then jerk back hard
to yank the canvas free and out
We stand and light our cigarettes

But then Cappo back there yells at us
Come on, let's get this lot all done!
He hands each of us a shopping-bag
a plastic supermarket one
Pick up every bit, he says
Don't give the buggers piss to find!

I kick through the black shit on the floor
these fuggin boots they hurt like hell.

Do you see the Tower of Skulls
                    the Cele Kula!
the Turk did that to us, a thousand heads
of serbs cut off to use for bricks
to show, if any proof was needed
how ruthlessness is efficient to its ends

Then in Kragojevik in 41
the Nazis gathered out of every school
a whole year's class one year of kids
... and handed to each child a spade to dig
a trench into that earth so long and deep
that in the silence when it had been filled
the raw earth has never been still since

Cruelness owns no people, has no creed
it is a lesson that their history has taught.

That day, behind the old man's chicken shed
I held the small hen's jerking feet
as he squeezed its beak to choke its squawks
hauling hard back on the neck until it broke
and sprang up on itself, a gristled thing
arched like a stiffened cock that spurted red
as the head fell soft, eyes lizarding to death

The picture of it's stuck here in my mind
like dogshit sticks fast to your shoe
and can never be wipe clean enough to rid
all traces of its last remaining stink.

Tell me, she said, where did you get that scar?

Her fingers ran like water down my back
around the edges of the cicatrice
and down my back and down my back again
until it seemed their tenderness was like
the gentle movement of the surgeon's knife
parting the skin with just a little sting

and all the rest would happen in my mind

All these years he carved his angels
little girls whose shoulders sprouted wings
each feather lifted lightly from the next
as if a breath of wind would make them rise
without effort off the weathered bench
where in their shining virgin wood
each carving stood to be admired
before paint and gilding was laid on

With no thought then of what an angel was
other than a return for time and craft
he imbued them with a gentleness of grace
a rest their carving echoed in his heart
smoothing the roughness of his farmer's life

dirt dung and blood
clogged day to day. A year
when no disaster fell
was counted fortunate... the year
some broken thing could not be mended
was ridden with a little loss of faith
a further sagging of his shoulders
time now in everything became erosion

One thing only stood by him
when nothing new could be believed
that first bright showing of the wood
as bark curled back, its cool smooth
tissue here beneath his hand
coming in to being...